Behind
THE MASK

Adolescents in Hiding

Behind THE MASK

Adolescents in Hiding

Dennis Rozema

iUniverse, Inc.
Bloomington

Behind the Mask
Adolescents in Hiding

Copyright © 2011 Dennis Rozema

iUniverse books may be ordered through booksellers or by contacting:

iUniverse
1663 Liberty Drive
Bloomington, IN 47403
www.iuniverse.com
1-800-Authors (1-800-288-4677)

ISBN: 978-1-4502-8357-1 (pbk)
ISBN: 978-1-4502-8359-5 (cloth)
ISBN: 978-1-4502-8358-8 (ebk)

Printed in the United States of America

iUniverse rev. date: 1/20/2011

To Trish and Meghan,
your love and your words live on,
helping others.

With knowledge comes understanding;
With understanding comes truth;
With truth comes love and forgiveness;
With love and forgiveness,
There is a light that erases the mask.

Disclaimer

The information, ideas, and suggestions in this book are not intended as a substitute for professional advice. Before following any suggestions contained in this book, you should consult your personal physician or mental health professional. Neither the author nor the publisher shall be liable or responsible for any loss or damage that allegedly arises as a consequence of the use or application of any information or suggestions in this book.

Contents

Preface

3/16/2010

If you are an adolescent dealing with depression, anxiety, or suicidal thoughts, you know about living behind a mask. You also know you need something to change. Perhaps that is why you picked up this book.

If you're the parent or friend of someone dealing with these issues, you want to help, but you may not be sure how to help. What you will find in the following pages will not only help you to understand the issues being dealt with, but also teaches you skills that will make a difference.

My name is Dennis Rozema, and I am the author of *Behind the Mask*. I have yet to type the first words, and before I start, I'd like to explain whom I am writing to, why I decided to write *Behind the Mask,* and what I hope you get from reading it.

I have worked with adolescents, their families, and their friends for my entire adult life. I have learned to appreciate the tremendous difference that a caring family and friends can make when they really understand the issues that are being dealt with. They can then effectively help loved ones who are using a mask to avoid dealing with the issues that threaten them. It is for the troubled adolescent, and for the family and friends who love them that *Behind the Mask* is written.

The idea to write a book came to me years ago while I was reading the journal of a former student I was very close to. She had recently committed suicide, and her older sister had encouraged me to read her journal. The journal had been kept during the six months before my former student died. As I read, I found that she referred to me a lot. Although it was difficult to read, it was obvious that she cared about me—as I did about her—a great deal. She was an extremely intelligent, caring person with great insight and humor. Her journal showed excellent insight into the mind of someone who was seriously depressed and suicidal.

Because her sister wanted to keep the journal itself, I made a copy and have had it for years. In it was written, "If I die, give this book to Dennis."

It is my belief that quotes from that journal and from other writings I have been given over the years will make an excellent book to help others better understand depression and gain insight into how we can help ourselves or those we love let go of the mask. Letting go of that mask helps reveal our true selves and allows us to live happier and more fulfilling lives.

As you read, you will see quotes from four different individuals. They are included by topic rather than by individual. One series of quotes may come from several different people. Different formatting and quotations will be used to separate their writing from mine.

For more than twenty-five years, I have been a school counselor, the crisis counselor for a school district, and an adolescent therapist. During that time, I have been blessed to have been given journals, notes, letters, and comments from the adolescents I have worked with. These students have been my best education. They have taught me how to be a better therapist, friend, and parent. Overall, I know my experiences with these kids have made me a better person. I am very grateful to all of them. It is from these experiences that I hope to help you understand not only the person who lives behind the mask but also how to reach out to him and give him the help he's looking for.

I have learned from my experiences that the person others and I see from day to day is not always the person struggling behind the mask the person wears. Their writings, which so honestly describe their thoughts and feelings, do a much better job than I ever could of explaining the difficulties of growing up while facing life's problems. I may have observed, and I hope, helped them along the way, but these adolescents lived it, and through their writing they explain the truth of what it is like behind the mask.

When I started thinking about this book and the masks that adolescents wear, I realized that there was certainly more than one kind of mask. Masks come in as many different forms as people come in different forms. We all come from different cultures. Even if the culture is the same, families live it in different ways, so every family is, in reality, a different culture of its own. And these different cultures deal with mental health problems in different ways. But depression is still depression. The feeling is the same, even if people have different masks and different behaviors.

No matter how different they may be, masks seem to boil down into three categories. What I think of as the cheerful mask is used by someone who feels a wide range of different negative emotions about herself, her life, and the situations in which she lives. She doesn't want anyone to know the hurt, fear, depression, and anger that live inside her. She doesn't even want to reveal it to herself. To protect herself from feeling and dealing with those emotions, she acts like everything is fine. She appears to have a personality that is outgoing, cheerful, and friendly. To those of us living with her, that is who she is.

Sometimes, instead of an outgoing, personable exterior, a second type of mask is used: the neutral mask. This mask doesn't show much emotion at all. These neutral masks appear neither happy nor sad, and consequently, those who wear it are not well-known by others. They quietly blend in and purposely don't attract much attention. They are often intelligent. As students, they usually get good grades. They are most often quiet and polite, so their behavior attracts little attention from their parents, teachers, or peers.

As an educator for many years in middle school, high school, and college, I realized that there are many invisible students in our classrooms. They don't outwardly participate either in class or outside of it. They seem to prefer to be left alone. Since they are doing well and not causing any problems, most people leave them alone. Some teachers recognize that these are the students to reach out to, and these teachers try to get to know them better. With large numbers of students and busy schedules, that seldom happens.

> *"I got an A on my chemistry test today. It is amazing to me that no one really knows who I am."*
> *"I may seem like a happy kid, but every morning, I slip on this fucking outfit that*

*makes me out to be fine, but it's a fucking
fib, and I've gotten good at fucking hiding
it—hiding my anxiety, my grief, and lack
of interest in other people's shit. I don't
know who this person is."*

These kids certainly don't have good perceptions of themselves
behind their masks. They assume that what others see in them is what
they see in themselves. When they are told that they are liked, they don't
really believe it. They only see what they see in themselves, no matter
what others say they see. It makes it hard for them to understand, and
they wonder what the truth really is.

*"I guess I long to know what others think
when they see me: passersby in the hallway,
my classmates, teachers, even my best
friends. Do they see what I see, or do they
see what I act like I want them to see? Are
my own perceptions of myself accurate?
Rarely does a day go by when I don't
change my view of myself. Some days, I'm
ugly, hideous—a huge head with distorted
features and an odd, misshapen body.
Other days, I'm completely acceptable. I'd
much rather be me than anyone else. Still
other days, I border even on pretty—clear
blue eyes, ivory skin, and a nice mouth
with a nicely proportioned small figure.
Only one of these can be what is truly
there, because last I heard, we don't morph
into other forms on a day-to-day basis."*

On the other extreme is the third mask, the angry, defiant mask.
This mask is worn by kids who act out the hurt, fear, and anger that
lives inside them. They definitely get noticed. There is little doubt about
what others think of them. Other angry, hurt kids identify with them,
and they bond together. Most adults and many kids observe how they

act and believe they are bad kids. We don't think of the angry, defiant adolescent often enough as someone wearing a mask. For the most part, they are loving and compassionate kids who don't know how to handle the difficult circumstances into which they have been thrust. Eventually, they act angry for so long that they don't really know a different way to behave. They know they are capable of loving and being loved. Yet, they also feel so hurt and horrible inside. They don't believe they deserve love, so they act in a way that drives others away.

> *"I'm a fat, ugly whore. I know it; they know it; and so they can all just go to hell."*

Over the years, I have gained some insight about the people who lived behind their masks. It's my hope to pass that knowledge on to you. Whether you are the adolescent yourself or a parent or friend who just wants to understand better, it is my hope that *Behind the Mask* helps you to understand and learn more about helping yourself or others to let go of the mask and become the people they were born to be. I hope these quotes and my narrations about those quotes will help you understand more about:

- the despair that lies behind the mask;
- the emotions and behavior that fuel that despair;
- the relationship of the mask to addictions;
- how love and trust leads to hope and recovery; and
- how someone can be the person who makes that recovery possible.

Understanding is only the beginning, so I also hope to help people learn how to deal with these kids and their masks in more helpful and productive ways. They have the right to hide, if they choose. But, in my experience, most of them would prefer to live a more fulfilling life and are just waiting for the right person and time to help them step out from behind the mask. You can be that person!

I intend to keep any identifying information out of both what these adolescents have written and my comments. Except for my own name, there may be blanks where names were used. I may fix some, but not all, of the spelling and grammar of their quotes. Things were often written in times of great anguish, and the individuals were not always sober while they wrote. This typing is a lot easier to read than some of their writing was.

I can guarantee that the writings are honest. At the time these quotes were written, the adolescents were not thinking about a book. They just wanted to express themselves and try to figure out what was going on inside.

I've written my narrations in the first person. I want to speak personally to you. If you're reading this, then it is written to you from me and from the nameless adolescents who have shared their thoughts and emotions. It is my hope that this book gives you, the reader, some knowledge and understanding of what and who is behind the mask. Hopefully then, with that knowledge and understanding, you will better understand how to help remove either your own mask or someone else's mask.

Acknowledgments

I recognized years ago how much devotion, passion, and tenderness it takes to be effective—not just as a therapist but in all aspects of life. I have tried to put those qualities into my writing. So most importantly, I want to recognize you—those whose names are confidential—who have taught me those qualities and have contributed to this book. Because of the love you have given back to me, I have that devotion, passion, and tenderness. The words "Thank you" sound like small words, but I know that you know how important they are. —Thank you!

PART 1:
People Like Me:
Who Wears the Mask?

We all do. We wear masks and act differently in different situations. I do. When I was an adolescent, I certainly did. I acted differently around my parents' friends than I did around my own. We all conform to certain expectations in certain situations. However, "people like me" know, or they think they know, that they really are different. They know better than to let anyone else see what they believe about themselves.

One particular student I worked with often referred to herself, both in writing and in person, as "people like me." I would often find notes that had been written the night before waiting for me on my desk. One particular day, the note included the following sentence.

> *"Well, it's getting late, and 'people like me' should be in bed early. So take care. I hope to see you soon."*

Whether or not they are any different from anyone else doesn't really matter. The fact is they feel different. They look at the world around them and think that everyone else is fine and that it is only they who are so unlikable.

> *"I hate myself so much. I am repulsed by*

> *myself. I feel fat, ugly, gross, sickening,*
> *hateable, and not to mention, crazy and*
> *strange."*
> *"I'm just a slut brain."*

Why else would they wear a mask if not to keep others from seeing who they see as themselves? Letting someone get to know them the way they see themselves is dangerous. They believe they are unworthy of the compassion and love we all need. If someone knew what was inside, these adolescents believe that, at best, they would never get the love they need. At worst, they would be seen as crazy and be locked up somewhere.

> *"I guess I feel that sometimes being too*
> *honest can be dangerous to people like me.*
> *I don't want to end up in that hospital*
> *again."*

Everyone's mask is different, but the masks have a lot of similarities. Hurt, anger, fear, depression, alcohol and drug use, and a perceived loss of love are all common to most kids' masks.

HURT
Where It All Started

"It hurts so much when all you want is someone to care that you're crying hysterically, helplessly, that your life is a mess, and they don't. All I want is someone to care."

The mask didn't just show up one day. It grew over time. It may have developed over a short time, or it may have taken years, but it started growing in the past. And it usually started because of some kind of hurt that was experienced. There are a lot of ways to be hurt, but if the adolescent doesn't deal with that hurt, the result is the same. She ends up with pain so deep that it makes her want to hide. Hiding seems necessary at the time, and the best way to hide and still appear to be okay is to hide her hurt behind a mask.

When someone is hurt, is in pain, or has experienced trauma, she eventually feels anger. The anger is there because she has not expressed the pain. When you just think about it on a small scale, it becomes obvious how this works. If someone has his new bike stolen when he is five, he cries. He may even get angry. But if he never cries and holds it all in, his anger would eventually grow. As more hurt happens, which it does for all of us, he learns to just keep hiding it. As he grows older and deals with larger hurts, he has to either let it go or form the mask that hides it. The larger the hurt, the more important it seems to hide it.

Many people experience trauma in their lives. If someone has learned to hide his feelings, it is because the trauma he experienced becomes something important to hide. I have known kids who have completely fallen apart because their girlfriend or boyfriend of two weeks broke up with them. At other times, I have known kids who have suffered through unimaginable difficulties and had the skills to deal with it well. It is not the people on the outside of an event that determine it was traumatic; it is the person who experiences it that makes that determination.

Trauma and other hurt come in a lot of forms, and it builds on itself. Experiencing a painful event causes pain. Thinking in negative ways about the event and its pain leads to feeling anger. The troubled adolescent can hide the anger and hurt or act it out. Acting out the anger inappropriately causes more negative events, which cause more pain, and on and on it goes. Hiding the hurt leads to the cheerful or neutral mask. Acting the anger out creates the angry, defiant mask. How the adolescent thinks about and perceives events is the key to understanding and learning to let go of the mask. I will talk a lot about thinking later in the book. Some examples of trauma, hurt, and pain and the thinking that goes with them are quoted below.

> *"I've kissed two cousins and have slept with my brother. I was between 8 and 10 years old. Gosh, I've been waiting to say that out loud for so so so long. One time, we made a tent under the ping-pong table, and another time, we did it in one of our box forts. Wow. The more I write, the angrier I get. Who teaches this shit?"*

> *"Everything good is so temporary, and all the shit, the bad stuff, is permanent. It hurts so much when all you want is someone to care that you're crying hysterically, helplessly, that your life is a mess, and they don't. All I want is someone to care."*

> *"I can't stop thinking about her. I have to accept that she is no longer here, but I can't. I can't let her go. The more I think,*

the harder it gets, but I can't stop. What's wrong with me? Everyone else seems okay, and here I am all fucked up. The only relief is when I'm high."

"He asked the right questions today. I can't tell him. I hate to lie. He has been so good to me, but if he knew what happened, what would he think of me then?"

Hurt needs to be expressed. When it is expressed through inappropriate anger, it leads to more hurt. Expressing anger in constructive ways allows the anger to dissipate, but it may not allow someone to understand and express the hurt. Being willing and able to actually talk about and experience the hurt gives that person the ability to actually let the hurt go. I understand it is not an easy task, but with the proper help from family and friends, it does happen. When family and friends are not enough, it is time to seek more professional help. Without that help, hurt and anger spiral downward until the person is depressed.

ANGER
Lies between Hurt and Depression

> *"The angry me is very much awake. I'm starting to listen to what it is saying to me too. I think the angry part of me is right: I should self-destruct."*

Anger and Violence

Hurt may be what lies behind the anger, but it is often anger that people see. Anger can be kept behind the mask, or it can *be* the mask that hides the hurt. When the anger gets expressed, it usually causes more hurt due to the consequences of angry behavior. This cycle of hurt causing anger and anger causing hurt builds until the person loses the ability to think calmly enough to make any kind of positive change.

> *"There must be a very angry person on the inside of me that wants to release its fury but doesn't want to hurt someone else so it attacks itself, which is me. The problem is that I don't know how to calm this angry person down. I don't know how to get in touch with that person. And I have to find out soon before it manages to self-destruct."*

This is one of the quotes that helped me realize how much the person behind the mask could help others understand what it is like to live that life. Obviously, this is a very angry person, but at the same time, I know she was a very intelligent and compassionate young lady. How frustrating it must have been for her to feel such rage and not know how to deal with it, to want relief but not to want to harm herself or anyone else. So many times, I have seen how frightened kids are when they don't know what they might be capable of doing. They can actually see themselves in the horrible stories they see on the news. I have been told more than once how scary it is that they can understand how school shootings could happen.

Some of those kids are just angry, violent individuals who are not wearing a mask at all. They are wired differently. The angry, violent person people see on the outside is no different from the sociopath who lives on the inside. The adolescents I am talking about in this book—the ones wearing a mask—look like sociopaths, but they are wired the same way any of us are. When they perceive having been attacked or hurt, they strike back. As adolescents without fully developed brains and usually little parenting to help them, they don't know how to constructively act their feelings out.

> *"I don't care. I hate them all. They don't care about me. Why should I give a shit about them? I wish they were all dead. I could kill them all!!! If you put a gun in my hand, I swear I would do it."*

It can be hard to know the difference between, whether an angry adolescent is depressed, or is acting out more as a sociopath. How often have we found out after a violent incident that the person who committed the violence was known to be depressed and either was in or had been in therapy? It is easy to look at that from the outside and think that someone didn't know what she was doing. "Why was that kid allowed to be free if they knew what he was capable of?" It is not my place to get into a debate about the right and wrong of any of those situations. However, I will say that I know it is a very fine line. It's very difficult to know when someone will actually act out. As with the suicidal adolescent, it is important to listen carefully. When a loved one has reason to be concerned, he should ask for help. Even professionals ask other professionals for their opinions in these kinds of situations. The loved one shouldn't take on himself all the responsibility for these potentially dangerous kids. Whether they threaten suicide or violence, no one wants to end up feeling responsible for what could potentially happen.

I often encourage clients to write: about their anger or other feelings, about what was happening when they felt those feelings, and about how they acted out their feelings. You're reading some of that writing as you go through this book. When someone starts getting specific in their writings by naming people they want to hurt or by describing in detail what they want to do, they are crossing a line that needs to be addressed—just like when the suicidal person has a plan and knows when, where, and how he will kill himself. Loved ones need to react. Kids need to make sure someone—an adult they trust—knows what is going on. Adults need to make sure a professional knows what is going on. Then a proper evaluation can be made to determine how serious the situation is and what the appropriate response should be. Taking advantage of your school's counseling department can be a good place to start letting someone know what is going on and what your concerns are.

Some kids can write some pretty scary things.

> *"So don't be surprised when I hit your kids*
> *with my fist. What's a conscience? I don't*
> *even know what the fuck that is. I'll kill*
> *you and chop you up into little bits."*

When what the troubled adolescent has written scares himself, as it usually does when he reads it over, he should ask for help.

> *"Am I normal? I can't believe the fucked*
> *up shit I write. Obviously, I need help."*

Statistically, this kind of violence rarely happens. But it does happen. This points out again why it is so important to listen and understand what is behind the troubled adolescent's mask. When the adolescent is understood, people can help themselves or others let go of the mask and learn to trust and love again.

Taking Anger Out on Themselves

Anger comes from being hurt. The anger that leads to shootings is often related to hurt from being bullied. The victim of the bullying has a person, or people, or place to direct their anger toward. The anger other depressed kids feel is no different, except it usually comes from the past. They know it is not fair to take it out on others. Sometimes they believe their only alternative is to take it out on themselves.

> *"As for me, I'm depressed, I'm drunk all the time, and most of all, I'm going nowhere but down quick. I have no one to blame but myself."*

In the last several years, cutting has become a more and more common way to express these angry emotions. Some think this behavior is a suicide attempt. Most often, that is not the case at all. Cutting is usually an expression of emotion. The adolescent believes that those emotions cannot be let out in any other way. Although not the only emotion, anger is a common source of this urge to cut.

> *"I just ripped open my arm again. I did not use a knife to cut it; I just ripped off the scab. It's bloody. I hate to be this, but I am so pissed off, and there is a definite part of me that would love to take a knife and rip the hell out of my arm."*

It may be hard to understand, but often, cutting is seen by the cutter as a positive thing. It releases emotion, and the pain actually feels good.

> *"I feel very much like cutting my arm again. I really am sick, that doesn't seem like a 'normal' person. Why would I enjoy hurting myself? I hate it, but I like how it makes me feel. I really am fucked up."*

When cutting does not make things better, which it never will, something different has to happen. That angry person has to find a way out. One way to stop feeling anger is to stop feeling at all: make that final decision and end a life that seems to be only painful.

> *"The angry person is very awake inside of me. It makes me feel like tossing it all away. I mean, like, make a real and true attempt—and I would succeed if I tried. I can't get it out by speaking. It only seems to come out when I take a knife to myself. Maybe that would be better. I don't know. I feel so fucked up, I can barely stand it."*

> *"The angry part of me keeps trying to persuade me to do it. Maybe I will. Maybe I won't."*

A better solution for dealing with all this anger is to better understand the hurt that causes it and then let it out in a safer and more constructive way.

Cutting and other forms of self-destructive behavior seem to help in the short-term, but in the long-term, these behaviors only make everything worse. Other behaviors such as punching pillows, pounding on beds, or punching bags offer less destructive ways of being angry. Even just talking and crying will help release the hurt beneath the anger and make the child feel better without the added pain and guilt.

> *"I talked about _____ today. Don't know why. But it just got around to that, because every time I get depressed, everything comes back to _____, and that's what I've been thinking about. I guess, deep down, that's a big part of my problem."*

> *"I find myself feeling more up than I*

*have been for a while. I think because I
acknowledge my anger. I think the more
I let out, the happier I will feel if I let it
out constructively."*

Anger Wears People Down and Leads to Numbness

Often people who are so angry and depressed feel worn down. It takes a tremendous amount of energy to be so angry and keep holding it in. Most depressed people will describe themselves as tired all the time. Instead of facing life, they would rather just sleep. They may try to wear their masks of normalcy or happiness, but they can't hide their exhaustion.

*"I couldn't go to school again today. I just
can't get up. I told my mom that I felt sick,
but I think she is catching on. I can't go
on like this. Someone is going to figure me
out, and I can't let that happen."*

Sometimes that worn down feeling becomes so overwhelming that all that is left is numbness.

*"I'm going numb, or at least I'd like to
think so, because nobody's body can feel
this pain like I do."*

I hope you can see the relationship between the pain, the anger, and the numbness. The pain and the anger build on each other and lead to numbness. The more pain he feels, the angrier he feels. When he inappropriately expresses his anger, he causes himself more pain. That self-inflected pain comes from the internal and external consequences of his actions. That just leads to more anger. Eventually, some people have to feel numb to stop that cycle from continuing. Numbness is just another form of the mask that is trying to protect him from himself. Numbness can be brought on by the adolescent's own mind, or it can be brought on through external means, like using alcohol and drugs to feel numb. Alcohol and drug use will be talked about in more detail later.

At the core of all that anger is actually the pain and hurt from the past. To effectively deal with the anger, he has to actually deal with the hurt that causes it. He certainly needs to learn how to constructively express anger. But to let the anger go, he has to understand its origins and let go of the hurt that caused it. For most people, that is a lot harder than it sounds. Being angry seems to work just fine—that is, until the consequences mount up. When someone finally wants to deal with that angry person, he finds himself having to deal with the hurt person behind it.

DEPRESSION
Spiraling Down

"If I keep this up, I am going to end up living on the street with nothing."

Think about the times you have been hurt. You most likely cried or got angry or both. If you were to hold it in, because you had learned at a younger age not to deal with those feelings, the feelings wouldn't go away. They would just stay inside and build up. As other hurtful things happened, emotions would build up more.

When someone holds in a lot of pain, anger, and fear, he almost has to become depressed. It's the holding in and building up of such negative feelings that create the need for a mask. That mask keeps others from knowing and keeps the person behind the mask from having to deal with the feelings. The energy to maintain that mask drains him and leads into depression. Feeling depressed is not pleasant. I guess that's kind of obvious, but ask anyone who is even moderately depressed, and she will tell you how much she hates it and how much it takes out of her life.

"I hate this. I go round and round and never really get better. I can't stand feeling like this. It is no wonder I want to die."

"Just everything really sucks so much! And I don't even have any more tears."

"Shit, I already feel dead, but I'm alive. I want to weep, but I can't cry."

13

Crying Is Healthy

When someone is sad, a normal response is to cry. Crying shows that he is sad. If he isn't letting anyone know his feelings, he can only cry by himself. If he cries by himself, he is admitting to himself that he is sad. The whole purpose of the mask is not only to keep others from knowing how he feels but also to protect himself from the truth that he knows is there.

> *"I just feel down, like I'm going to start*
> *to cry. I never really cry. I can't let myself,*
> *but the tears fill my eyes sometimes."*

Crying is one of the best ways to let out pain. It is an honest expression of hurt and pain. Because a person is able to cry, he is less likely to become angry, which leads to greater problems. It is easy for us on the outside to say it's okay and good to cry, but it is a lot harder for the person feeling the pain to allow himself to do it.

Holding Feelings In Wears People Out

If the adolescent behind the mask thought someone saw how they really felt or who they believe they are in there, they could not live with that. So they have to hide those horrible feelings and perceptions of themselves. Keeping up that mask requires so much energy that it wears them down. They get so tired of pretending and they just want to give up, which becomes another feeling they have to hide.

> *"I'm tired of hurting. I'm tired of pain.*
> *I'm tired of trying. I'm tired. Let me be*
> *free. Let me go. Let me die."*

Without help, depression is like a constant weight that can never be gotten rid of. It is always there. But still they smile, laugh, go to work or school, and appear normal. I have seen so many excellent, well-liked students, whom you would never guess, are depressed or drinking and doing drugs excessively. Without change, they just slip deeper and deeper into depression. Behind their masks live people who can barely maintain the strength to keep up their facades. When they get so tired and depressed that they can't keep it up, they are forced to either continue to struggle, give up and die, or ask for help.

> *"I just wish it was over. I need some time without pressure so that I can get a strong foothold on life. Right now I hate it so. And yes, I wish I were dead."*

> *"I wish I could restart my life, but I'm way too deep in this shit to now start over new. I know I need help, but how do I tell anyone now what's going on?"*

When the troubled adolescent doesn't tell anyone, she starts to believe she'll never get better. Even when she does tell someone or gets help, problems don't change easily or quickly. One of the classic signs that a person is suicidal is a sense of hopelessness. That hopelessness comes when the person feels like she's kept trying and trying, and nothing seems to help. She's so tired and apathetic that she just wants to give up.

> *"I don't want to die. But there is that part of me that is so tired. So tired. Tired of feeling the hurt and pain and the helplessness (like when it will be over?). Maybe that is hopelessness. Not much difference anymore."*

The Decision to Die Is Not an Easy One

The fear of death and the guilt that comes from thinking about suicide are strong. If a person were to die, how many of the people who love him would be hurt? So the desire to live and get better is also strong. When a person is suicidal, it doesn't mean he has no concern about the ones he loves. Even though he can't stand living like this anymore, he doesn't want to hurt the ones who have loved him. This is often the heaviest weight in this balance between living and dying.

> *"I wish to die, and no one except myself*
> *can stop me. But then how come everyone*
> *would be so hurt?"*

Maintaining that balance becomes so confusing that he often feels guilty about the way he thinks. He feels all this pain, and yet he looks around and sees people caring about him, and he doesn't understand why. That confusion and guilt just makes him more depressed. He blames himself for the hurt he causes the people around him. He wants to feel better, but he doesn't know how to get from where he is to where he wants to be.

> *"It is strange, because that keeps echoing*
> *through my mind. Life is good, and I don't*
> *know why I keep wishing to be dead."*

> *"I have no right to be like this. I should*
> *be up. It's long past the time for me to be*
> *over with this and to move on. Why can't*
> *I move on? I don't understand why I can't*
> *leave my problems in yesterday."*

> *"This is one hellhole of a shitty day. I've*
> *had more than I can take with these meds*
> *for depression and anxiety, and look at my*
> *current state: I'm ten below the sea. I'm*
> *drowning, and I can hardly breathe or*
> *even open my mouth to scream, and just*
> *when I am near unconsciousness to get*
> *relief, I wake up and realize that it was*
> *all only a dream, which stinks, because*
> *my dream is better than reality. This,*
> *unfortunately, is the life I lead."*

There are times when these kids just about give up. There are times when they do give up and actually make an attempt. At first, these attempts are usually not very life-threatening. The kids are often testing their ability to follow through and putting others on notice that their pain is real. They are trying to say that they can't stand it anymore. If a friend trusts that she can wait and see if the adolescent actually makes an attempt, it could be a deadly mistake. Some kids, especially boys, can be very impulsive. This is why you see suicide situations in which no one really had any idea the person was suicidal. I'll say it again. If, you the reader, suspect someone, or know yourself to be suicidal, ask for help.

> *"My mind is hating me for not giving up already, but don't worry, brain, you're about to get some relief, because we're going to get to sleep for the rest of eternity."*

> *"Well, I made it. I didn't even take another Xanax. Maybe if I told someone what I did, then they would understand I REALLY WANT TO DIE."*

> *"Suicidal plans are starting to band together in my mind, because life's a fucking scam, and I am going to end mine."*

> *"Nothing more to do.*
> *"Nothing more to say.*
> *"Nothing more to live for."*

Hospitalization

When the troubled adolescent becomes hopeless, no longer wanting to try, she starts making real attempts. If she survives those attempts, hospitalization usually becomes necessary. When a friend or loved one can't trust that a person will not harm herself or another, a line is crossed. Making a real attempt crosses that line. Not only do people have a moral obligation to be sure that person is protected, but those responsible for the child also have a legal obligation. That being said, short-term hospitalization is not always a good thing. One would think that the fear of being sent to the hospital would keep the adolescent from trying again. Sometimes that is true.

> *"I must confess that I have thought of taking a lot of my meds. But I would end up in the hospital again, and I couldn't handle that. But then again, that is only if I fail."*

Often, I have found that being in the hospital, itself, provides little long-term help. It can, however, be the beginning of a process that leads to long-term help. Effective follow-up needs to take place. Some of the best clients I have worked with I see for the first time after a hospitalization or a return from a treatment center. I find them to be much more motivated, both because they don't want to return to the hospital, and because they truly have learned that they need help.

Some kids find that the hospital is safe. They are away from all the disruption that was caused by themselves, their family, friends, and school.

> *"Well, I just got out of the mental hospital. What can I say? Not a whole hell of a lot and, then again, probably a lot. I wish I could live there. It's so perfect, so sheltered. They protect you, and you think you're okay because you do so well in there—not even do well, I actually fucking thrived. And you think you're better and you're going to do so well and that fresh start crap, and making changes, and then you get out and everything is totally awful, and you're worse off than you were when you went into the hospital. You realize that you don't really want to make changes, but you have no choice, and your whole life is in other people's hands. You have no control. And all your friends treat you*

> *like, at any second, you're going to haul*
> *off and go nuts on them, and your mother*
> *acts like you don't deserve anything and*
> *takes everything away from you. I want*
> *to fucking go back there."*

Unfortunately, sometimes being in the hospital scares the troubled adolescent into being less honest. He is trapped between two conflicting desires. He wants to get better and knows he needs to talk about his feelings to get there. He also knows that he wants to die and that, when he talks about that, he is afraid he will be sent to, or back to, the hospital.

> *"I am afraid to deal with my feelings,*
> *because I don't know what will happen*
> *if I do. I am afraid not to deal with my*
> *feelings, because I am afraid of what*
> *will happen if I don't. I am really caught*
> *between a rock and a hard place."*

It is hard to listen to the pain that comes with a person who wants to take his own life. I have known counselors who, as soon as the word suicide comes up—*bam*—he would be out of the office and in a hospital. After that kind of experience, it is hard for the adolescent to trust again. Now I have to be careful here, because I don't want to give the impression that hospitalizing an adolescent is the wrong thing to do. The problem is that there is such a fine line between accepting someone's feelings as normal for his situation and knowing when he has crossed that line and he has to be kept safe.

Knowing When to Ask for Help

This book is not meant to be a training manual for suicide prevention, but I know from my own experience that listening, understanding, and not overreacting to what is heard is important. There is a big difference between not liking living a certain way and really wanting to die. In order to understand that difference, people need to be able to ask the right questions and really listen to the answers. The important questions revolve around the person's:

- intention of actually doing something to herself (does she have a plan?);
- means of doing it (does she have a way of fulfilling the plan?);
- time when she would do it (does her plan include a when?); and a
- place where she would do it (is that in her plan?).

There is a big difference between saying, "I can't stand living like this anymore," and saying, "I am going to kill myself with my dad's gun Sunday while my family is at church and I'm up in my bedroom."

Someone should ask questions such as "on a scale from one to ten, how strongly do feel you want to die?"; "If you were to do it, how would you do it?"; "Do you have the pills you would need?"; "When would be a good time to do it?"; "Where would you do it?" Obviously, the more certainty with which someone answers these questions, the more serious the situation is for them. If the person asking is not sure, it is always best to error on the safe side. The hospital will do its own evaluation and decide if hospitalization is in the person's best interest.

People should trust their instincts but not let themselves get so close that they lose their objectivity. This is especially true the closer they are to the person. Parents or friends can find it hard to be objective. They should be a good listener and understand what the adolescent is feeling. But when they are uncomfortable, it is time for them to talk to someone else. It is important to get a more objective view of the situation. Calling a school counselor or trusted clergy member is always a good idea. When anyone feels that discomfort, they should encourage or even force their friend or loved one to seek professional help.

This seems like the right time to talk about the confidentiality that friends have between each other. Most kids trust their friends much more than most adults, because they know that they can count on their friends to keep secrets. I can't stress enough that this is *not* the time to be keeping secrets. If someone is concerned about a friend or even not sure if he should be concerned, he must talk to some adult that he trusts and be honest about what is going on.

The vast majority of suicidal kids I have dealt with over the years have come to my attention because of a caring friend. The friends have come because they wanted to know if their concerns were justified. They wanted to know how to help or where to seek help. Friends are almost always concerned about their friends finding out who told. Honestly, their friends will probably figure it out, but their friendship will survive, because their friend will survive. In almost every case in which I have been involved, the friendship not only survived but got stronger! The suicidal person appreciated her friend for helping to make something that was helpful finally happen.

ALCOHOL AND DRUG USE
It Feels Right for a While,
But It Only Makes Everything Worse

> *"As for me, I'm depressed, I'm drunk all the time, and most of all, I'm going nowhere but down quick."*

My point about alcohol and drugs is not as much about the addiction to those drugs as it is about the relationship they have with depression. Someone could write and entire book on drug and alcohol addiction; and many have. I include substance use here because, first, it correlates to depression so strongly, and second, the use of alcohol and other drugs comes up often in the journals, letters, and notes I have seen.

> *"Friday, Dennis told me I shouldn't drink, because if I do, I might commit suicide. When I'm sober, I'm safer than when drunk. Now after a few beers, I think he's right."*

Drugs Do Make Kids Feel Differently
Many of the drugs kids use, including alcohol, are depressants—not a good thing to be using when they are already depressed! However, it's pretty hard to argue that using substances does not make an individual feel better at the time of use. One of the biggest problems with any drug use is that the drug *does* provide what it's advertised as providing. I won't say that the feeling is always better, because sometimes using

can be pretty scary. But it does make the user feel differently than he did. Feeling differently is usually the objective.

> *"I want to spend the summer the good way, the way summer should be. I mean, this year, we're going to go to big parties, smoke pot, and get drunk. God, I can hardly wait. And I also want to get on _____ again. I don't know why, but it makes me feel good, and I just do."*

But like I said, it is not always a good feeling, especially after the fact.

> *"Or I could say that I was incredibly stupid to get drunk and high and suck 3 guys' dicks in the bathroom and practically get raped. I could say that, definitely. I don't even know what to think about it. I could think so many things. Like, take any point of view. I am so dumb! I didn't think so at the time, but now everybody knows, and I don't know what they all think, but I know they don't expect it, and I look like the biggest fool, and nobody is going to leave me alone for a long time."*

Behavior like that is a pretty big consequence. The decisions made while under the influence of a substance usually cause regrettable results.

> *"The ticket last night—82/55 DWLS, no proof of insurance—what the fuck? Plus, open beer, more drugs, beer, shrooms. And I'm getting my shit together?"*

"I've been drinking too much lately. I'm starting to lose things: money, clothes, makeup—all that good stuff."

"Do I Have a Problem?"

As those consequences mount up, the user starts to wonder if maybe she does have a problem. She may never admit it anywhere else, but she starts to get worried about what the truth may be.

"I, in part, want to stop drinking because I'm beginning to wonder about it. I have a part that says, "a few beers here and there won't hurt you." I'm going to get myself in deep with this one if I don't stay and/or get in control."

"I fear my drinking, and yes, I think I have a problem. I'm not saying I have a drinking problem. I have a problem with my drinking. And I'm scared. Don't let me become an alcoholic. Don't let me become an alcoholic. Don't let me become an alcoholic. Am I already, even now?

"I hate how I always think I'm going to accomplish great things, and it just never happens. I am just a big loser who can never do anything I say I'm going to. I will be a slacker for the rest of my life. I will listen to music and think and talk on the phone and hang out with my friends and talk about all the wonderful things I want to do, and the only thing I'll ever be is an uneducated chain-smoker living it up with the cockroaches in my low-rent apartment."

Drinking, or any drug use, and depression become partners in a cycle that leads deeper and deeper into both a substance abuse problem and more serious depression.

> *"As for me, I'm depressed, I'm drunk all*
> *the time, and most of all,*
> *I'm going nowhere but down quick."*

Sometimes this cycle of use just leads to believing the problem is caused by what the person is using, so all the user has to do is stop using that particular drug and continue with or start using something else. It sure doesn't seem logical to anyone looking in from the outside, but to the user, that thinking has nothing to do with logic. It has to do with keeping up the mask, and using does that just fine.

> *"I am on my way to getting my shit*
> *together. I cut back on the drugs. NO*
> *COCAINE! Pot's alright, and beer has*
> *to slow down."*

I have found that most of the suicides and suicide attempts I have dealt with were attempted when the person was either drinking or under the influence of some other drug.

> *"I'm so fucked up. It would be so easy*
> *now. I really don't care if I live or if I die.*
> *What difference would it really make?"*

Denial Is Part of the Mask

Denial is a classic component of any negative behavior that someone wants to keep hidden. Very seldom does someone easily admit when he has a problem. It doesn't matter if the problem is drug use or depression. Not every adolescent, or adult for that matter, who has depression has a problem with substances. However, anyone with either a problem with depression or with alcohol and drug use is likely to be in denial. Although it certainly has happened, seldom has someone voluntarily come up to me and said, "I have a drinking problem that is making my depression worse. Can you help me?"

> *"I don't care what anyone thinks. The way I feel is that I'm going to get drunk whenever the fuck I want and do anything I want with whoever I want for no other reason than it's fun. And I will smoke as much pot as I want and get high as a fuckin' kite. And they can all say I'm fucked up and a slut, but what matters is that I know I'm not, and so do my friends."*

"And so do my friends"—now there is a justification for keeping up negative behavior. Friends are great to have. We all need them. But a real friend can look at someone and his behavior objectively and confront him with what he is doing to himself. They will help him look at the mask and try to break through his denial. I am asking that friends be real friends!

When a person is in denial, the mask gets stronger. If anyone tries to get through that mask, the person behind it often gets angry. The person behind the mask uses that anger to push a friend away. As soon as the friend gets angry back, the person behind the mask wins. He now has more reason to believe his anger is justified, and the friend has been pushed away from the truth. When good friends and family care, they are able to see what is going on. They know this behavior is a desire to hide what lies behind the mask, and I hope, they don't get angry back. The best reaction is for friends and family to stay calm and consistent. They should point out what they see, let the person behind the mask know they understand but that they still want that person to face the truth.

That friend or parent shouldn't let the troubled adolescent's anger stop her from being that consistent person. Sometimes she has to be gentle, and sometimes she has to be really tough, but she always has to be consistent and keep looking for the person she knows is behind the mask.

> *"All these people claim to know what's best for me, but they don't even know anything about it. They weren't there, and they don't know how I feel. I just want everyone to stay out of it."*

> *"Maybe I have changed, but this is me. And I like it."*

> *"I truly hate her. If I want to do something, I'll do it, and I fucking don't care what she thinks. As soon as I can, I'm going to get so fucking stoned, and then everything will be so cool, and then I can hang out with my friends, and it will be so much fun, and she can go to hell."*

Denial is the purpose of the mask. The person uses denial to protect himself from his own feelings or when he is trying to protect his substance use. The use of substances with a depressed person is most often a means of protection so he doesn't have to actually face his feelings. It never works in the long-term, and it only makes things worse. Unfortunately, the long-term is not the concern. Protecting his feelings now is all that seems to matter.

> *"He said I shouldn't drink. I have had a beer. Either way, if I do or don't drink, I end up feeling like Mom. I might as well use booze to numb the pain."*

Self-Medication
One of the peculiar things about substances and depression is that doctors, pediatricians, and psychiatrists often prescribe medications, which are legal substances, as treatment for depression, anxiety, and other mental health disorders. Kids will use these legal substances, as well as illegal sugstances, in an illegal and dangerous way for the same

end result. They want to feel different and not feel their pain. As far as the kids are concerned, they think their own prescription does a better job. That way they can keep their mask and continue using without anyone checking up on them.

> *"I went to my shrink, and she wants to put me on medication. No way. She can kiss my ass. She tried to make my friend take it, but she won't. It's dumb. Like, no way am I going to be all weird and unnaturally mellow all the time. No, thank you. I'll smoke pot if I want that."*

It Doesn't Work Forever

Eventually—often sooner rather than later—the troubled adolescent starts to lose control of her use. When it doesn't have the same effect, it seems to make sense to try more or other substances. Eventually those substances don't work either. That cycle keeps happening until she gets into trouble because of her drug or alcohol use. She deepens her denial, which causes her to use more. She eventually starts to realize, "This isn't working."

> *"My life is not worth jack shit. I hate my life so much. My mom has somehow found out about me smoking pot in town and who we get it from. I hate her. She is threatening to send me to boarding school, and my life is hell. How does she find out about this stuff?"*

> *"You know what really sucks? How I haven't really had any real feelings about anything for a while."*

> *"Either you have fun and have a life, or you can think and figure yourself out, but not both. That kind of sucks. Maybe I just*

> *need to figure out the middle and do that.*
> *I'm confused about so many things right*
> *now, and I don't know where to start to*
> *figure it out. So right now, I'm not going*
> *to. I'm going to go to bed."*

What Is and Is Not Peer Pressure?

One last thing I would like to discuss about substance use is the concept of peer pressure. I hope most people don't still believe that there is some bad person out there pressuring their children into using. No one is out there telling them that they will not be "cool" if they don't use. Kids use mostly for two reasons: They like it, and they trust that it will work.

At first, they are just curious. It's available. So they decide to try it. Peer pressure has nothing to do with it. Pressure to use doesn't come from external sources. It comes from internal thoughts. They don't want to be left out or be different. No one makes them do it. They want to try it. Even the fact that they may not like it the first time is not enough to overcome the internal desire to do what others are doing. It is their own feeling out of place that pressures them. What makes it worse is that, if you have problems in your life, drug use becomes what seems like a great way to avoid those problems. Having problems makes the desire to use even stronger. The more they avoid the problems, the worse they get. The worse they get, the more the kids want to use. You can see how it just keeps growing from there.

> *"I really dislike alcohol. Well, sort of. I*
> *don't think I'm ever going to be a real*
> *big drinker. I thought beer was supposed*
> *to make you, like, hyper. It put me to*
> *sleep."*

> *"They understand nothing, and I swear*
> *they think that the only people who do*
> *drugs or smoke or whatever are, like,*
> *fucked up losers who are greasy and gross.*
> *And it's not true, because they don't get*
> *it that so many people do that shit just*

because it's the way we are for no real reason. We just are."

"And it's not like we pressure each other. It's our own decision, and we don't need to impress anyone or anything. God, I hate parents. I wish me and my friends could run away."

FEAR
Formed in the Past, Living in the Present

"I am afraid to deal with my feelings, because I don't know what will happen if I do. I am afraid not to deal with my feelings, because I am afraid of what will happen if I don't. I am really caught between a rock and a hard place."

We all know fear. Things happen that scare us. Normally when we are scared, we act out that fear. We scream, yell, or maybe cry. Sometimes what scared us keeps us from reacting. We are afraid that our reaction will cause more of what scared us in the first place. That may be appropriate at that time. It might be true that our reactions could cause more of a problem. A girl who is molested by an older sibling or her uncle or her father could understandably go numb and not act out her fear. Striking back in that type of situation may cause a more serious reaction back on her. Although that reaction is understandable at the time, it sets a pattern of behavior that will cause a lot more problems in the future.

Fear from the Past
Most of the kids who live behind a mask live in fear that their secrets will be found out; that everyone will know what they did, or what happened, or who they think they are.

"Molest—to accost and harass sexually. Thank you American Heritage. I cannot accept that. I can't believe I was molested. There is a small part of me that wonders

31

what happened. Like I know but can't put it in words."

"I feel very alone, in a bad way. Not lonely and not the usual alone but an alone that is total fear of those around me. I don't even feel like I can trust Dennis, and that's sad. He's a man. I can't just ask him not to be."

Fear and trust are on opposite ends of the same situation. Fear keeps a person from trusting, and trusting can create fear. This happens when someone trusts people that have hurt them. The trust someone fears is in the present, but the fear itself comes from the past. It was a loss of trust in the past that caused the fear in the first place. I guess it is always something from the past that starts the formation of the mask. Once that formation starts, it builds on itself. The troubled adolescent believes he's hopeless, so he acts like he's hopeless. Those actions make him feel even more hopeless. It's a cycle that continues downward until he hits some kind of bottom, which helps him break the cycle. Everyone's bottom is different. I've known some kids who have had what seemed to be very few consequences change their behavior. I've known others who have nearly died several times and still not change anything. While they are sliding down, they usually know inside what is going on.

"As for me, I'm depressed, I'm drunk all the time, and most of all, I'm going nowhere but down quick."

"To me, I know what's best for myself, and you can't focus when you're all fucked up all the time. No wonder I have no money. I'm a lush!!!"

Fear in the Present
The other fear I find to be true so often has to do with facing the people who know the troubled adolescent the best and care about her the most.

Once she starts opening up, she's taking the risk that the person she trusts will start learning more, and if that person learns too much, her secret will be out.

> *"I don't know what I am going to say to Dennis. If he asks how I am, I will selectively tell him the truth. If he asks direct questions, I will refuse to answer if my answer could incriminate me. I will try not to see him any more than I have to. I'm not going to see him every day I am there anymore, because I will be there every day. He is the biggest threat to my security. He did it once [I had her hospitalized], and yes, I'm afraid he will do it again."*

Once she's trusted others enough to open up to them about the truth of what lies behind the mask, she's taking the risk that the information can be used against her. She has spent so long protecting herself that it is hard to trust others with the truth.

> *"There is so much I want to say, but I am unable. I am trapped behind my walls of protection, and they are closing in on me."*

> *"He talked about men today, and NO WAY! NO WAY!"*

It is not hard to make assumptions from that short statement. And you would be correct about most of what you would think. There can be very strong reasons to hold on to a mask that protects the troubled adolescent from the fear that lives inside.

Fear Protected Them in the Past,
But Trust Lets Them Live in the Future

Some things are very difficult to face, but when the troubled adolescent trusts enough, he can get past the fear and accept that it will be safe to relate it. Then progress can be made. It starts slow, but eventually over time, the reasons for the fear all comes out.

> *"I still am very confused. I don't know what to do. I think I might ask him for his trust and safety and whatnot. And if I feel secure enough, I will explain everything. Everything."*

Fear is a wall that protects. The fear helps create the mask and maintains that protection. What is eventually learned is that the same mask that protects a person isolates him. It keeps him from growing, forgiving, and loving. It keeps him from being loved, which is what he needs to be whole again. In the meantime, he's trapped between what he sees as two choices that are both bad.

> *"So here I am: too young to die but too cold and weak and tired to live. I don't know at this point what shall become of me. If I were to die, it would be a waste of the gift of life, which is short to begin with. If I were to live, it would be too painful to bear."*

> *"I'm afraid to take the road to life, because my real feelings would come out, and that would be very uncomfortable for me to deal with openly."*

The mask that was built was needed when the events that created the fear happened. As the troubled adolescent grows past those events, the mask hurts more than it helps. Still, letting go of the mask is a very real risk. There are no guarantees that he will never be hurt again. In fact, he most likely will get hurt. But letting go of the mask and trusting again gives him the skills he needs to deal with future events in his life.

The Fear of Living

Another of the fears a suicidal person lives with is not so much the fear of dying but the fear of not dying.

> *"I must confess that I have thought of taking a lot of my meds. But I would end up in the hospital again, and I couldn't handle that. But then again, that is only if I fail."*

Normally, when someone fails to kill herself, it would seem that the fact she is alive is a gift. Often, that is the case. She does realize there is another opportunity to start over and, this time, get better. Just as often, however, she is disappointed and, secretly, more determined than ever to make sure she will not fail the next time.

> *"Next time, I will do it right."*

It May Have to Get Worse Before It Gets Better

Knowing that someone one wants to kill themselves sounds pretty scary. But the truth is that most people, adolescents included, have to come to a point at which they know they have to fix what is wrong. They have to want to stop going around and around and finally do something different. That doesn't happen until the consequences of their behaviors pile up to the point that they realize they have to change. Until that happens, it is a lot more tempting to just give up.

> *"I can't take this shit anymore. No one understands. Don't they realize I JUST WANT TO DIE?"*

It's sad that it has to happen this way, but the more someone gets into trouble, the more he finally starts to realize that it is he who has to change and not everyone he keeps blaming for his problems. Like many therapists, I see many clients a few times, and then they stop coming. They aren't really invested in making any changes.

But when they come back, it is after they have gotten another minor in possession, or been hospitalized, or been suspended again from school. That is when they are more willing to look at themselves and the behaviors that got them into those situations. When they agree to look at themselves, they can replace their fears of themselves and others with acceptance and love for themselves and others. Often, it was a loss of trust and love that caused the fear. Letting go of the fear makes room for the trust and love they need.

THE LOSS OF LOVE
Perception Is More Important than Reality

> *"But tonight, I wrote down what it was to love, and in doing so, I gave Love meaning, and when I realized that, I realized my reason to live is love."*

As I stated earlier, we all wear masks, but I learned early in my career that truly depressed and troubled teens wear a much stronger mask and hide deeper behind the mask than the rest of us. Only slowly, if ever, do they reveal what is hidden behind it. Once revealed and understood, these troubled adolescents are the strongest, most intelligent, loving, and compassionate kids you will ever know. They have lost trust and love, which created their masks. Learning to trust, be loved, and love again dissolves the mask and reveals that the true person wants the love and warmth she has been missing.

So many people with problems have had love taken from them. It could be as simple as losing a girl- or boyfriend when they are particularly vulnerable or as complex has having been raped or molested by people they trusted. It could be the death of a child or a parent or even a succession of deaths. Whatever the cause, when someone loses his ability to love and accept love, he is much more likely to lose his desire to live. Being loved and loving again bring back the desire to live.

> *"It is such a cold world that we live in, and when we try to warm our hearts and lives with love, this world snuffs it out like a candle, and the world becomes an even colder place. It would be better to*

not know the warmth of love at all. But it is the warmth of love that gives this life in this cold world its meaning. With love, there is excruciating pain and suffering and the shock of facing the cold reality of this world. Without love, there is only pain and more pain with no relief until we are overcome and are taken out with the mercy of death to another, as of yet unknown, existence."

"When I was really down, nothing seemed to matter. To me, there was no difference between life and death, and love did not seem to exist (It existed, I think; it just seemed meaningless), and because it all was meaningless, there seemed no reason to live and go on with this life. But tonight, I wrote down what it was to love, and in doing so, I gave love meaning, and when I realized that, I realized my reason to live is love. So I want to thank you first of all for your love and support and for your helping to teach me what it means to love. I know what it is to love again. Life really is empty and meaningless without it. I'm not going to let myself lose the meaning again."

Love Has Different Meanings

Love and the phrase "I love you" are very loaded with different meanings in different situations. It has always been my belief that you cannot be helped, nor can you help, if you do not love yourself, love others, and accept the love of others. I am reminded of a Beatles song from the sixties that includes the words, "All You Need Is Love." It is certainly not that simple, but loving and knowing that you're loved surely helps!

As a professional, I understand all the legal and therapeutic reasons to be careful expressing yourself. It is important that your expression of love not be misunderstood. But love, when honest and taken as genuine, is often what makes the difference between therapeutic success and failure. The love of a friend or a parent makes a difference! Love is a powerful force!

It is important to understand that love has to be perceived as love and then accepted. A depressed or addicted individual often has a hard time accepting that she is loved. She carries a lot of guilt and shame. Her reasons for feeling such self-hate are not entirely unfounded. She has done a lot of harmful things to herself and those who love her. This makes it hard for her to understand that she is still loveable.

It Wasn't That They Weren't Loved Enough

Too often, the parents or friends of someone attempting or achieving suicide feel a lot of guilt, because they believe they did not do enough or they did not love enough. That is usually not true. The love was there; it just couldn't be seen or accepted.

Someone reading this book may have been in that very situation. I have been there myself, along with so many parents, teachers, and friends who have lost people to suicide. I know it is hard to accept, but the person attempting or completing the suicide themselves made that decision. They may have blamed others, or they may have blamed themselves. Whatever their situations, they made the choice. And it was a choice made out of confusion and irrational thinking. It was not a decision made because of a lack of love from those around them.

I am truly sorry if you're the reader and have lost someone. But, please, don't blame yourself. If blaming yourself still bothers you enough that it interferes with your own recovery from your loss, it may be time to ask for some help for yourself.

CHOOSING LIFE
Instead of Choosing Death

"Death shall come and ask for my decision: life or death?"

Reasons for wearing the masks are as different as the people who wear them. When I was younger, after a few years of listening to problems, I felt like all the different problems were the same song being played over and over with either a different instrument or a different tune. I thought of my job as exciting—a game, like chess, in which I was manipulating the pieces and figuring out the strategies. I was helping to change that song from something sad to something joyful.

But then someone committed suicide!

A real person, whom I loved, actually died. Her death was permanent. It couldn't be changed. There were no longer any strategies, nor was there the ability to change her song.

I realized then that it never was a game. It was very real. I was not a chess master. I felt powerless. I had always been passionate about my work and had cared very much, but it didn't make enough difference. The suicide still happened.

It took some time, but I slowly recovered after that death. I became even more committed to making sure that I would always do everything I could to make sure that no one I dealt with would committee suicide again. At the same time, I also learned that, no matter what I did or how much I cared, the decision to live or die is within the other person. It's not in me or anyone else.

The journal of that person, the one who died, is one of those from which quotes in *Behind the Mask* are taken. She is one of the two people to whom this book is dedicated.

Don't Ignore Feelings

Unfortunately, she was not the last person I knew who would achieve suicide. If I hadn't learned already, I certainly did as time went on; anyone is capable of actually committing suicide. I will never believe someone is incapable of taking that last fatal step.

Some people still think that threats are just that: threats. They believe that it is wrong to give in to that kind of manipulation. It's true that most don't follow through, and sometimes, it is a manipulation. But when these kids do what they threaten to do, it is a devastating loss. When it is a manipulation, why would they be manipulating? They want someone to do something that will help them.

Many may think the troubled teen is threatening because of some simple irrelevant situation that the child is manipulating like if a parent won't let him go out that night, but I can assure you that there is more to it than that. If he is telling someone he will kill himself, the person listening needs to respond, to make sure he knows that the person making the statement knows he was heard. No, he still cannot go out that night, but there are problems going on that are more serious than being angry about not being able to go out. If or when he threatens, it is time for the friend or parent to ask for some advice from a professional who deals with depressed adolescents. I have told many parents to tell their kids, "If you are serious, then we need to get you some help. If I need to, I will take you myself or call the police and get you to a hospital. If you are not serious, don't try to play with my emotions. I love you, and I will not let anything happen to you. I will get us whatever help is needed." A key word in that statement is us. Most often it is not just the adolescent who needs help but the entire family.

A Decision Will Be Made

When someone is at the point of making threats or even just thinking about killing herself, she knows she has to make a decision. Often, she knows that death is not a real option, but she can't stand living the way she is living. When nothing seems to help, she starts to think differently—"Maybe death really is an option." As time goes on, she realizes more and more that a decision has to be made.

*"Death shall come and ask for my decision:
life or death?"*

Making the choice to die is a difficult one. It usually is not made quickly or without warning. Some depressed, suicidal individuals wear very good masks that they have built up over years. The masks have been reinforced, layer upon layer, as the adolescents repeat behaviors that confirm what they inaccurately perceive to be the truth. We have all heard the stories of people killing themselves with no warning. It does happen. But most give signs of what they are feeling. That is why people hear about the warning signs of suicide. There often are warning signs. "People like me" don't make that choice lightly, and until the end, they actually want help.

*"Everything is so confusing and depressing.
I just want to be happy. All I want is
someone to care."*

There are some traditional signs to look for, and if you are dealing with someone who is depressed and may be suicidal, it will be important to know what they are. Some of those signs are the answers to the following questions:
- Does the person have a family history of depression, suicide, or other mental health disorders?
- Has there been an event or series of events that would explain depression?
- Does the person verbalize his thoughts of suicide?
- Does he have a plan in mind as to how to commit suicide?
- Does he have the means to carry out that plan?
- Does he have a timeline as to when he would carry out the plan?

Obviously, the further you go down that list, the more serious the situation is. The friend or parent shouldn't be afraid to ask these kinds of questions. They are not going to give the troubled adolescent any ideas he doesn't already have. If the parent is concerned, then she should be seeking professional help to evaluate the situation and help decide what would be the best thing to do.

Often, these questions are never asked, and the adolescent feels like he is never heard or understood. Even the professionals don't always seem to get it right.

> *"I saw my therapist today. I tell him I feel very suicidal, and I ask him what I should do. He says, "Don't do it." Well, thanks a lot. No shit, don't do it."*

> *"I saw a new therapist today. She told me—quote—'I'm a therapist's worst nightmare.'"*

I'm not trying to make therapists look bad. I am one myself. But even therapists get frustrated and don't always listen to what they are told or, apparently, even to what they are saying themselves.

The original point I'm trying to make is that making the choice to kill oneself is confusing. It's not an easy decision. It is sometimes thought about for years before the adolescent either gets the help he needs, makes an attempt, or actually commits suicide. During that time, he will have let others know his thoughts, feelings, or even plans in some way. In the end, his depression makes death look more attractive than life.

> *"I may choose life, which is full of worry and stress and suffering, or I may choose death, which offers the chance for peace."*

> *"I wish I could restart my life, but I'm way too deep in this shit to now start over new."*

> *"Should I fully experience life before I fully experience death?"*

Everyone's story—or song, as I used to call it—is different. The stories may seem the same—"My parents are divorced"; "My father abused me"; "My mother died"—but loved ones have to listen carefully to understand their perceptions of the situation. The people behind those masks are individuals, with what may seem like the same problems as someone else, but their fears, or their traumas, or their depression, or their addictions, or whatever their issues, are theirs, individually and personally. The masks may also look the same, but they too are individual and personal. As scared as the troubled adolescent is, she needs someone to reach into the mask and acknowledge, understand, and love the individual who lives behind it.

> *"I find myself needing two things. The first thing I need is my space. A distance for my own protection, where I will be safe from being touched by anyone "physical sense". It would make me feel so incredibly awkward to be touched. But the second thing I need is to be held and comforted and just to hear that everything will be okay, over and over again. That would be so healing and also bonding for me. But I don't feel comfortable with that, I guess because I do not feel worthy or deserving of that. Yet, I know that I have a need for that, so what do I do?"*

Loved Ones Can Help Make the Right Decision

Who can give those two important things? The person reading this now. Anyone can be that person who reaches out, who listens and understands. Whether a parent or a friend, loved ones should remember that the person that they're dealing with is wearing a mask.

The loved ones need to look behind the mask and listen, show him they understand, and then tell him they care and that it will be alright.

The troubled adolescent needs to hear these words from loved ones. He needs to know they have listened and understand. Then he will listen to them, and they can help him find the help he needs. It is always important to listen first, if they want him to listen to them. That last sentence may be one of the most important lessons in this book. A person must listen first, if she wants to be listened to.

A previous quote mentioned touch. Like the quote implied, touch is something people have to be very careful about. Someone should only touch with permission. Someone who has been abused or has lost trust in some other way can be wary of being touched. Intruding on his space without permission will do much more harm than the good that normally comes from the compassion that is shown by touch. Yes, touch shows compassion and concern, but even with permission, touch is a sensitive issue. The point is serious. If a person can't be sure how a touch will be interpreted, then that person should not be giving hugs or touching shoulders or arms. I believe that touch is an important way to communicate concern and compassion, but again, people need to know how it is going to be interpreted. This is another form of "listen first." The loved one needs to be aware of what the troubled adolescent is telling him about touch and how she perceives it. That communication may be through words, or it may be through body language, but he needs to listen to what she is telling him.

Being patient with, listening to, and understanding what is behind someone's mask is not easy. Hopefully, as the reader reads on and hears the voices from behind these masks, he will come to know that he can make a difference.

What makes understanding important is related in the progression of the following five quotes.

> *"I'm digging myself a hole, and unfortunately, it's a grave."*

> *"I wish I understood feelings and how they work."*

> *"I wish to experience love, life, and security before I fully experience death."*

> *"I am in serious trouble, and I must save myself, and I will."*

*"It was so cool. He listened to what I said.
I think he understands. Maybe I should
trust him???"*

*"I am starting over. It feels good… I plan
to take good care of myself physically,
mentally, and spiritually again."*

That wasn't the first, or the last, time that the last person quoted started over. The journey out of depression can be a long and frustrating one for everyone involved. There are many ups and downs. The troubled adolescent living with these problems often feels like she's living on a roller coaster. She's constantly going up and down, feeling good and then feeling bad. When she's feeling good, she's afraid she'll soon feel bad. When she's down, it's hard to believe she will ever feel better.

*"The freaky thing is that the mood changes
are every few minutes. I am getting
motion sickness from being up and down
so much."*

*"What really bugs me is that I feel like I've
gone around in a circle, and now I'm just
about back to where I started."*

Taking Care of Themselves First
It's not just the depressed person who goes up and down or around and around. The people around her who love and care about her also get dragged along. When they're dealing with someone in this situation, it is important for them to keep themselves stable and balanced. It is hard, but they have to know that the worst thing they can do is let themselves get lost in someone else's emotional roller coaster. They can't let her life consume them. They should do what they can to help, but they must keep themselves somewhat separated. They should find other outlets for themselves. If it gets so hard that they find their own emotions affecting their lives, it may be time to look for help for themselves. They shouldn't be afraid to ask for it. They don't have to do this alone.

PART 2:

Help, Hope, and Recovery

"Nobody can help me but myself."

No matter where or how a person looks for help, in the end, it is that person's own work that makes things better. As a therapist, I certainly believe in getting some help to do that work. It is a lot of hard work. Look at what has been included so far. Coming out of all that fear, anger, and depression is not easy. It takes a lot of honesty and trust and a willingness to make hard choices and changes in order to make someone's life better.

It also takes a lot of time. Recovery can be very elusive. Someone can think he's there, and suddenly, it slips away. I've known so many students and clients who have repeatedly made progress before something out of their control spirals them back into their old thinking and behaviors. It happens a lot with substance abuse, but it is just as common with depression or anxiety or any other mental health issue.

Relapsing back behind the old mask and into the behaviors that went with it is frequently caused by events out of the person's control. He may have changed, but the world around him is still the same. The same pressures, the same family, the same friends are all still there. Often, these were the reasons that led to his problems in the first place. When they are still part of his life and they have not changed, it is hard to maintain the changes he wants to make.

Other times, however, these events are not something out of his control but something he does. Actually, it is always something he does; whether the initial trigger is external or internal, he is supposed to be in control of the decisions he makes. Making a wrong choice or being in the wrong place can easily set him back.

Eventually, with enough experience, he will learn what triggers to avoid, including the wrong choices and the wrong places. Facing those ups and downs is the start of a recovery, but those ups and downs get confusing. One day, the troubled adolescent knows he's on the right track, and the next, he feels those same old feelings. The resulting confusion can actually be a good thing. It starts him thinking. If he's thinking instead of just acting and reacting, he can start to look at things in a new way.

CONFUSION
Starting Recovery

> *"I don't understand. Life and Death. It goes round and round. I do, and then I don't. I am so confused. Do I really want to die or do I really want to live?"*

What Makes Dealing with the Mask Confusing?

When the troubled adolescent knows she needs help, it is just the beginning. Most people's masks are very thick and strong. It is easier to hide behind the mask than it is to try and break through it.

> *"There is so much I want to say, but I am unable. I am trapped behind my walls of protection, and they are closing in on me."*

The troubled adolescent doesn't just one day wake up, know she needs help, accept it, do all that work, and get better. It takes a lot of time, consequences, trust, confrontation, awareness, and acceptance to get to that point. For some, getting to that point comes easily. For others, it may never come. For most, it takes time. I have noticed that the first signs of wanting help are ambivalence and confusion about the choices that have been made and are still being made.

> *"I may choose life, which is full of worry and stress and suffering, or I may choose death, which offers the chance for peace."*

"I am confused when I choose to die and take my life. My life becomes peaceful and calm, patiently waiting for death to come at its right time. When I choose life and turn from death, I am overcome by the urge to take my life. I do not understand. I want to be better, but is it worth it?"

"Should I fully experience life before I fully experience death?"

"As I stand in my indecision, I remember what I wrote previously. 'Death shall come and ask for my decision: life or death.' My decision will be in my indecision. Death will take me. Maybe that doesn't have to be. Maybe I can make the decision to live."

Because they are confused and not sure what they want, troubled adolescents aren't always exactly honest, or they are very careful about how they say what they say. They may be telling the truth, but they may interpret a loved one's question differently than that person meant it.

"You will say that I lied to you when I told you I was okay, but I did not really. We just have different definitions of okay. To me, okay is having a way out if one is needed and also accepting it if it is to be. I was okay."

They are okay because they know what they want to do, and they believe they are comfortable with that decision. At least at the time, they are comfortable. At another time, they are not okay and want to let everything out, but they are still scared. They trust, but they have been hurt so many times. They don't want to hurt anyone else; they know how that feels. All these conflicting feelings make it hard to stay behind the mask, but it's just as hard to let someone else see what is there. It is so confusing that they often just do nothing.

> "There is so much I want to ask you
> and tell you that I don't know where
> to begin. So I don't begin at all. I just
> remain silent, not knowing what to do. I
> lose then, because who knows how long I
> will have here, and that is an opportunity
> lost forever. There would be so much left
> unsaid if we should be forever parted, and
> I would have wasted the chance to know
> you better, to explain to you how I feel
> about you. Just so I know that you know.
> You are important to me. I want to be
> able to be there for you just as you have
> always been there for me. I thank you for
> that. You hold a place in my heart that no
> one else can fill or even get close to. I save
> all our memories there, and when I am
> sad or lonely, I take them out to treasure.
> Thank you for being a part of my life. I
> love you. When I am down, I talk to you,
> and you always bring me up. When I am
> confused, I ask what you think, because
> I believe in you. When I am happy, I
> want to share it with you, so I can see
> your smile. When I know sorrow, I come
> crying to you, and you hold and comfort
> me. When life becomes too big for me,
> you help me put it in perspective. When
> I can't seem to see the obvious answers to
> my problems, you have patience with me.
> When I try to run away from life, you
> gently remind me to take responsibility for
> myself. When I take things too seriously,
> you help me to laugh at them. When I can

see only dark shadows ahead, you remind
me that then there must be light. When I
carry a burden, you help me shoulder it.
So, when the time comes that our paths
must take separate turns, remember I
need you, and one day, I want to be able
to do the same for you. I will never forget
what you have done for me. Thank you,
my friend."

Confronting Confusion

It takes a combination of asking the right questions and, more importantly, understanding when listening to the answers. Just being there for the troubled adolescent is helpful, but that's not enough to help someone change. A loved one certainly has to be positive. He doesn't want to reinforce the troubled adolescent's hopelessness, but at the same time, he needs to confront her with what he sees as the truth behind her mask. Listening helps him understand. His understanding by itself doesn't help her much. She needs to understand, and often, he needs to confront her with what he believes the truth is. He trusts her to be honest with him. Well, he needs to be honest too. She trusts him for that.

Confrontations are delicate and difficult, but she does have to learn to take responsibility for herself and her actions. He needs to balance being comforting and being direct at the same time. It is the understanding that he helps her to realize that will lead to her learning that she no longer needs her mask. This happens as trust is slowly built up. When she knows he cares about her and wants what is best for her, she will not only let him behind the mask, but she will let him confront it with her.

"I thought, 'He really knows me better
than I thought he did.' I was amazed and
almost, for an instant, thought the story
would all come out. It was difficult in
a way, but I managed to control myself.

I didn't want to get myself in any more trouble. Forgive me."

"Then we talked about all the weird thoughts I'd been having, like Uncle _____ and Dad. I told him of my fear that I would fall and destruct before I had a chance to progress again. I talked of my trying to push it away. He reminded me it was over."

"I'm starting to believe it really is over, and I will never have to go 'through' it again in the physical sense. I will have to work it through, but I won't be in those situations again."

TRUST
It's Their First Step

*"I told him everything. Everything. I took
a chance, but it didn't backfire."*

Trust is a lot like love in that it has to be real. It the troubled adolescent is going to be helped, he has to trust the person he is working with, be it a friend, a parent, or a professional. That person needs to be trustworthy and needs to trust you as well. Trust is something that is earned through behavior that proves the person can be trusted. Without taking that first step of trusting someone, no other steps in the right direction will follow.

So many times, kids put their trust in the wrong hands. It is so common for kids to gravitate to the wrong group of friends, just because it is easier and more comfortable than trying to make friends with people who don't seem to understand or like them.

*"They are all such a bunch of bitchy snobs.
I don't need them for friends anyway. They
can go fuck themselves. That's what they
all do anyway, the sluts."*

It seems like adults are the ones whom kids with masks trust the least. Adults threaten the kids' masks the most. Adults have authority and control, so they are feared, because they may force their way in and find out the secrets the kids are trying to hide.

I remember one case in particular. I had to call protective services because of a father who was sexually molesting one of the students I was working with. It was very difficult for her, but she agreed to tell the protective services case worker everything. The case worker made a promise he knew he couldn't keep. He promised he would not tell her father what she said. The next day, her father confronted her with everything she had told the worker. Then she refused to cooperate with protective services, and they had to drop the case. She also refused to talk to me for about a year. She did, however, stop seeing her dad.

If the case worker had been honest about what was going to happen, telling her that her father would eventually have to be confronted and explaining why and encouraging her that it would work out, it would have worked much better. Being honest builds trust. Obviously, not being honest destroys it.

Eventually, she started talking to me again, and she started seeing a therapist. Now she is a healthy, productive young lady. It does not always work out so well. Once an untrusting person trusts again and is hurt again, she often never trusts again.

Building trust is critical to allowing someone to open up. It does take time, but the sooner she starts trusting again and allowing trust, the sooner she starts feeling better.

"My world has changed so much in the last day and a half, so very much. From the beginning, yesterday second hour, I talked to Dennis, and I told him everything. Everything. I took a chance, but it didn't backfire. It was something I had to do, but it was painful within me. Dennis expressed his feelings about it, which was good.

"We had a very good talk about anger and what to do about it, or with it, actually. Dennis even said it was one of the best talks we ever had. It was so neat and helpful. I was so high or happy or whatever you want to call it. I hadn't felt so good for a long time. I gave him my sleeping pills and said, 'I don't need these. Please take them for me.'"

When trust is built, and the troubled adolescent is able to express the truth, he starts to understand himself and his situation better. He learns to start thinking differently and looks at himself and his situation with a different, better attitude.

AWARENESS
Learning To Think a New Way

"Sometimes, I wonder what I need to get over and through this. Sometimes, I think I should be forced to talk until I have nothing left inside me. Then sometimes, I think I just need someone to shake me into today and to tell me to quit being such a brat."

Asking for help is never easy. When the troubled adolescent asks for help and starts to trust, he becomes vulnerable. He may not understand all that is going on inside, but he knows it's painful. If someone starts asking the right questions, he will want to tell the truth, but at the same time, he believes the truth will hurt. It takes a lot of time, patience, and understanding to build enough faith that it is okay to be that vulnerable. Allowing himself to have that vulnerability leaves him open to the possibly that maybe his perception has been wrong; what others and his past life experience have taught him may have been wrong. Maybe there are other ways of looking at what has happened. Now, with better understanding, he can look at things differently.

"I must learn to keep things in their proper perspectives. My reality is distorted because my thinking is distorted."

I cannot express strongly enough the importance of thinking and the need to change patterns of thinking. When an event happens, we react to it. Let's say a kid has not been getting along with his dad, and

and his friends ask his dad if they can go out. His dad tells him how
bad he has been and that there is no way he's going out that night. The
kid yells back and stomps out of the room. He goes up to his own room,
slams the door, and punches a hole in his wall.

There is a lot more to that scenario than just those events, and
thinking is the key to changing the outcome. Let's break the event down
into specific pieces.

1. The boy in the story has done something to upset his dad.
2. His dad reacts in a way that embarrasses and hurts the feelings
   of his son.
3. The son has some thoughts about the event. He may even
   say his thoughts; perhaps, "You're such an asshole! You never
   understand, and you always embarrass me in front of my
   friends!"
4. When the boy thinks like that, he pretty much has to feel
   hurt. Feeling that hurt makes him angry.
5. When the boy feels that anger, he expresses it by stomping out,
   slamming the door, and hitting the wall.

When he's thinking angry, negative thoughts, he cannot help but
feel angry. He can't change the feeling. He feels what he feels. He can
learn to control his behavior, and controlling that kind of behavior is
certainly better than acting it out in ways that make things worse. But
controlling anger usually leads to a buildup of negative feelings, which
will eventually burst out. Sooner or later, he is going to express them.
That's why learning to express feelings in a positive, more productive
way is important. However, learning to think differently will keep you
from experiencing those feelings in the first place.

I have worked with enough clients to know how hard it is to change
someone's thinking, but the troubled adolescent can learn to change
his thinking. The boy in this story did something that made his dad
angry. If he was to take responsibility for that and his thinking was
more in line with taking responsibility, he would not have been as hurt.
He could have thought, "I didn't deserve that harsh a reaction, but I
understand why my dad is so pissed off." He might then have been able
to say something different, like, "Dad, I know I was wrong before, but
I've learned my lesson. Let me prove it by going out for just a little while

tonight." There is no guarantee that would have worked. But it sure has a better chance of working than what did happen.

In any situation, people have responsibility for their thoughts, for their feelings, and for what happens. The dad also could have acted differently, if he was thinking and feeling differently. In the story, the dad may have been thinking something like, "My son never gets it. He is always messing up. I can't believe he has the nerve to ask for any favors after he screwed up so badly." How does that feel to a parent? Would he feel disappointed, hurt, embarrassed? Feeling that way, again, is going to make someone angry. It is no different for an adult. If he feels anger, he's likely to say and do things he may regret.

Thinking in terms of absolutes like "always" and "never" makes it hard to be objective and look at a situation from a more neutral position. No one *always* screws up or *never* gets it right. A better way of thinking is to just deal with the situation at hand and be honest and realistic about it.

I hope it doesn't sound like I'm saying people should never be angry, because that is certainly not true. When someone does something that hurts someone else, that person is going to be hurt and is going to get angry. The things that person says to herself during that process determine how strongly she feels and how strongly she reacts. How she thinks is the part she has control over. She should use that control to help make situations better rather than letting her thinking and behavior make things worse. Catching herself and changing her thinking before she acts can make a tremendous difference in her ability to communicate effectively and to have better relationships.

Again, I know it is not easy, but if she pays attention to the way she's thinking, she can learn to look at situations in a way that will help her to feel better and then to communicate and act better. That's a good lesson for everyone—kids and adults alike.

LETTING GO OF THE MASK

With Love and Forgiveness,
There Is a Light That Erases the Mask

"I have to grow up and stop hiding."

Why Let Go

Becoming aware of himself and what he needs comes out of the trust and honesty the troubled adolescent has built up. The more he talks, the more he listens to himself, and the more he understands. The more he understands, the more he is able to think differently, and finally, the more he is able to forgive. Eventually, he starts to let go of the mask.

> *"I feel just like a little kid who has hidden out of fear and now is being called out, because it is safe now, and now is in need of being comforted. Just to hear, "It's over now. It's okay. You'll be alright, and you're safe now." Over and over again. I am not a little kid, not on the outside at least. I have to grow up and stop hiding."*

In the end there are only three ways for things to work out.

1. Death, sadly, is a real option.
2. Living with the mask and never dealing with it is another option. Some people make that work. Most are not very happy and don't live very fulfilling lives.
3. Choosing a mask-free, healthy life is the third option. When someone expects to live a better life and believes that she can,

she has a different attitude that allows for hope rather than despair.

"If I would kill myself now, it would be sad, very sad. I can't let that happen."

"I have come to the realization that a large part of my problem is that I have not been accepting one of the largest parts of life and that is death. I did not accept the death of _____ at all, and I have been doing my best to not accept _____'s death, which is a reality, a sad but true reality. I must allow myself to accept death and let that acceptance bring me peace and comfort. I must not only accept death for who it has already claimed but also for those who it may claim. I must be aware that death may take those I love and that there is nothing I can do but enjoy the time I have with them right now."

"No longer do I have to be afraid to love and lose, because I will make right now count, and if death shall claim someone I love, I will be comforted, because I made the most of the time we shared."

"I'm doing well, and I'm starting to have more ups than downs on this roller coaster of depression, so that makes me happy. I've been piecing myself back together slowly but surely with a lot of help from you and the hospital, and in fact, that is why I am writing you this very instant. I guess you could say I've made a breakthrough in all of this. But I could not have made it

if it weren't for the people like you in my life, so I want to thank you for what you taught me."

Forgiveness

I mentioned forgiveness a moment ago. It wasn't until I wrote that down that I realized how important forgiveness was to talk about. I am amazed that it wasn't in my original outline of the things I wanted to discuss. It is right there in the beginning of the book: "With Love and Forgiveness, There is a Light That Erases the Mask." So I went back through the journals and found this quote.

"I have to learn to let it go. I guess she did the best she could."

I think the best way I can express the importance of forgiveness is to relate a personal story about myself. At the end of my senior year of high school, my parents separated. They divorced during my freshman year of college. Like anyone's story, there certainly is a lot more to it than just those facts, but what's important is that I held a lot of resentment toward my dad. He had made a lot of mistakes, and my mom had finally had enough. Over the years, I had never really liked the way I had been treated by him. I had always felt like an object rather than like a loved son. The lack of love between my parents and my own feelings about that lack made for a very cold, unemotional place to grow up.

After the divorce, things were a lot different. My mom worked hard to fill the void I think she knew was there, but I had already moved on. I was in college and not home much, so I tried to just leave it all behind. Yes, I guess I was wearing my own mask. As I grew older and got into becoming a counselor/therapist, I realized how much my feelings toward my dad were interfering with my own ability to be a complete person, someone able to live in the present without having the past interfere.

Finally, I decided to confront my dad and try to talk over everything I felt was important for us to discuss. I actually tried several times, but he would never let that discussion happen. Eventually, I decided, with some help, that I had done everything I could to make things right. I also realized that my dad had done everything he could. He was who he was because he had grown up with the influences in his life. Those made him who he was. He never *tried* to hurt me. In fact, I know he loved me. He did the best he could. He did the best he could. Yes, I repeated that twice. It's important! From the time I realized that, I was able to forgive and let go of the resentment I had been holding onto.

A couple of years later, my dad died. I was then, and I still am, so thankful that I learned the lesson to forgive and let go before his death. Had I not done that, I may still be letting those old resentments interfere with my life today.

If the reader is someone hiding behind a mask, he should know that forgiveness may seem like an impossible thing to achieve, but it can be and is achieved. The process of forgiveness may start with confusion and ambivalence about the fear and hate the person feels, but with trust and openness in the right place and at the right time, that person will find the ability to think differently about his life and life overall. With new ways of thinking and the good feelings that come with those ways, there is a light that reveals the true person behind his mask. That, then, is the start of his recovery.

If the reader is reading this wanting to help those behind the mask, he should know that his listening, his understanding, and his love will be the keys to shining that light and helping someone on her journey into and through recovery.

RECOVERY
It Is a New Beginning, Not the End

*"Thank God I am out of that place. Now I can
start my life over without all the hassle."*

Most of the kids I have known have found the help they needed. Sometimes, it was their choice, and other times, they were convinced by parents or friends to seek that help. Either way it was help that led them to better understand their issues, the reasons why they had issues, and to develop the skills they needed to live their lives in healthier, more productive ways. One would think that would be the end of the story. That's not the case.

Whether recovery means being sober, feeling less depressed or anxious, or being able to maintain healthier relationships, recovery is the ongoing process of the awareness of the person's issues and keeping vigilant about the skills she has learned.

I certainly do not mean to imply that everyone needs to stay in therapy for life. I do mean to say that recovery is a process. It is a process that starts with getting help. It continues with, and then without, help until a structure and habits are developed that will continue throughout a lifetime. That process starts with acceptance.

Acceptance
Acceptance is when someone agrees to honestly engage herself in help. Honestly is the key word there. Many people enter therapy or start going to support groups or twelve-step meetings because they a forced to go. Being forced may work, but that force does not mean those people start out honestly engaged in the process. When they truly accept that they have a problem, they can then begin the process of their recovery. Some

64

people are in therapy for years, but their recovery doesn't really start until they truly accept that they have a problem.

Often, when someone leaves a treatment program or therapy too early, she thinks that she is done and that everything will turn out okay. So she stops her therapy, leaves the treatment center or hospital, and has no follow-up.

> *"Thank God I am out of that place. Now I can start my life over without all the hassle."*

Any skill we learn has to be practiced. Remember learning to ride a bike? At first, someone had to hold the seat and run along with us. Eventually they let us go. Usually not long after that, we fell. As we kept practicing, we got better, and eventually, we were off on our own. Recovery works the same way. A person has to keep working on it, even after she learns the skills.

Letting Go

Acceptance also means letting go, including letting go of the person she used to be and the mask she wore. After all the pain and hurt, that should be easy, but it is not easy at all. During the time of all that pain, good friends were made. They may not have been the best influences, but it seemed like they cared at the time. There was also a lot of fun had. Memories were made. Accepting that many of those memories and friendships caused more harm than good is hard. It is hard to let go of those memories and people.

She also learned to live her life a certain way. She was herself. She didn't always like it, but she believed it was better than the alternative. Being in recovery means letting that person go. It means letting go of the person she knows and has trusted, perhaps for years. People do it all the time—but not easily.

If someone is not letting go, that means there is still not an acceptance of the truth that so much harm was caused by their past. Letting go of that person, those other people, those places, and times from the past is perhaps the most difficult part of recovery.

She is not going to let go and keep practicing the skills she's learned unless she accepts that she can't do it on her own. To do that, she needs some kind of motivation.

> *"I'm home, and yea, I feel good, but I'm so scared. How the hell am I supposed to do this? Everyone is so excited and thinks everything is fine now. I know I can't just stay in my room, but I don't know if I can do this."*

Powerless versus Hopeless

One of the common themes in any twelve-step recovery program is the idea that a person must accept that he is powerless over his problem or his addiction. He needs faith in a higher power to help him deal with his situation. I personally don't disagree with that at all, but some people have problems with the ideas of both powerlessness and faith in a higher power. I would like to explain my concept of being powerless.

Addiction to any behavior and genetic predisposition to depression are both things people have no control over. So in a sense, people are powerless against the fact that they have those problems. The issue I have with the term *powerless* is that it implies hopelessness. The last thing someone who is depressed or addicted needs is to feel any more hopelessness. There is, in fact, a huge difference between powerless and hopeless. People have no control over the fact that they have a disease. It is not any different from having diabetes or any other genetic disease. That does not mean that they can do nothing to deal with the problem they were born with or the situation they have had to live in. If they don't effectively deal with the disease, it may kill them. That is just as true with addiction and depression as it is with diabetes or cancer. They have the choice, however, to deal with it. In that way, there is little difference between having diabetes and having depression. They can get the help they need. And, if they do, they can live very happy, productive lives.

That help can come in the form of faith in a higher power, the support of healthy friends and family, or the counseling of a trusted therapist. By far the most effective way to deal with depression is to take advantage of all those. People with depression may be powerless about the situations they found themselves in, but it is never hopeless unless they give into that powerlessness and quit trying to improve themselves. So they shouldn't quit trying!

Motivation

To maintain recovery there has to be some pretty strong motivation, because recovery is not easy. In most cases, a person who has made changes in his life still has the same external situations that gave him problems in the first place. If he was doing drugs, his friends are still doing drugs. When he was wearing a mask and acting like that angry, sullen kid, his friends were all feeling the same way he was. They still do. In most cases, the problems his family had, the family still has. Just because he has made changes does not mean that the world around him has changed.

Where does the motivation come from to stay in recovery and maintain the strength to keep that mask off? Remembering consequences is the strongest factor. A lot of bad decisions were made, and for many of those decisions, a heavy price was paid.

> *"I can't believe what has happened to me in the last two weeks. I nearly got raped. I got my second MIP. I almost died. Now I am getting out of the hospital only to probably go to jail."*

Remembering what the past was like and comparing that with what he has now can be the motivation to keep working and moving forward. There is no doubt that there have been a lot of good times, but he should ask himself, "Was it worth what happened, and do I really want to live it over again?"

> *"Life's so much better now. I don't know how I survived. I will never let myself go back."*

Another motivation is actually guilt. A lot of people who cared got hurt along the way. He can think of the friends who were lost and the ones who stuck by him, about the family members who are still there after all that was done to them. If he goes back to being that person again, he could lose them forever. Having that knowledge is motivation to keep the negatives out of his life and keep the positives he has developed within himself.

Having a Plan

I've known and worked with a lot of kids in recovery. Most of them no longer wore their masks and were motivated. They accepted that they needed further help to maintain recovery. I don't like using absolutes, because there are always exceptions. But I believe no one keeps off her mask of denial if she doesn't have some plan for maintaining her recovery.

Recovery after being in a hospital or treatment facility doesn't just happen by itself. It takes a plan. That plan requires goals, structure, support, and balance.

I would like to use the example of two young people I have had recent contact with: an eighteen-year-old girl and a nineteen-year-old boy. Both of these young people have very different stories, but they started at the same place.

While I was working for the school district, I ran recovery groups for students in recovery from substance abuse issues. Most of the kids had dual diagnoses, meaning that they suffered not only from a substance abuse problem but also from some other mental health disorder, usually depression. They were all examples of kids who had worn masks and were trying to live sober lives without the mask. My two examples were both part of this group during overlapping years.

The girl I mentioned was—on the outside—petite, cute, funny, creative, and intelligent. She had a family that loved her, and to a stranger, her life looked fine. In fact, under that mask, there was a scared, insecure little girl with little self-confidence. She got involved in drugs and thought that that was what gave her an identity that made her feel comfortable. The drug use got out of control, and she ended up in an out-of-state treatment program, which helped her a great deal. When she got home, she, her parents, the treatment program, and I set up a plan for her, which she followed.

This past summer I went to her high school graduation party. She has been sober for a year and a half. She is much more confident and has started college this fall. I am very proud of what she has accomplished, and I have great respect for her. Her journey may not be over, but she is well on her way to a happy and productive life.

The boy I mentioned I also respect a great deal. His story, however, is different. He was a part of the same group, but his drug problem was more severe. He was also dual diagnosed with depression and substance abuse. His parents have also been very supportive. He has been in counseling. He has been in several treatment programs and has spent time in a children's correctional facility. At every step of the way, he has been encouraged to follow a plan. When he was forced to follow—when he was locked in some kind of program—he would do fine. Not long after he would get out, he would put back on his macho mask and act like he didn't need the plan. Well, every time, he ended up back in trouble. Twice, he ended up in a hospital emergency room, either near death or having to be resuscitated back to life. I have not seen him in several months. I saw his mother a few days ago, and she let me know that, after being out of the house for a while, he has once again started over and is trying to get his life back together again.

He is also still on his journey. What will happen? I certainly don't know. I do know that nothing will change until he is willing to let go of that mask he wears and accept the structure, support, and love that is waiting for him. When he is willing to set goals for himself and follow through with those goals, he will start finding success.

Goals

Not having a goal keeps the troubled adolescent from having motivation. Goals don't have to be big long-term things like, "I want to have a certain career." Actually, those long-term goals, although necessary to keep in the back of the mind, are not as helpful as short-term goals. Often what is most important is having a short-term goal for what lies ahead each day: "I am going to be honest today and talk to my mom about how I feel about school." This is much more realistic and able to be accomplished. As he builds on short-term goals, the long-term goals become more possible. As he builds success in the short-term, he becomes more confident living without the mask.

One important daily goal he should have is to remind himself that this is going to be the day he makes good decisions. Those good decisions vary with each person, but if he wants to keep that mask off, he has to start and end every day with a goal and an evaluation of that goal.

Support

No one manages to live her life without the support of others. This is even truer when she is starting anew; trying to live a new life without that mask of protection she has been so used to.

Support can come in a lot of forms. Some of it is not always very good. Going back to her old friends who claim they understand her best and support her new ways may sound good. After all, they are her friends. They know her the best. They have always been there for her. She should take a little closer look at those beliefs.

"They know her the best"? They know the person she was, not the person she wants to be. I can guarantee that they want to keep her the same person she was. They don't want to change. Being with her while she's changed will remind them of all the mistakes they have made. It is much easier for them to change her than to change themselves. She needs the support of people who know and like the person she is now. It is hard to make new friends, but getting involved with new activities puts her with new people, who will get to know the new her. They will like and support that new her. This is one of the many good things about support groups and twelve-step programs.

"They have always been there for her"? Yep, they were there. They were there when she screwed up, and they covered up for her and kept her from the consequences that might have gotten her out of that lifestyle sooner than she got out. How much of the grief she's suffered could have been avoided if her friends had not been there for her? Support doesn't just mean people being there for her. It means people loving her enough to confront her. Often, it is the other people in her life who will see problems coming before she does. Making new connections and getting support from people who not only love her but will also confront her is critical while she's in recovery.

Balance

Balance is another critical component to recovery. While the troubled adolescent was wearing the mask, life was completely out of balance. Nearly all his effort was put into maintaining the mask and the life that went along with it. Now that the mask is no longer there, the areas of life that were ignored have to be recovered. It is recovery not just from a mental health or substance abuse problem but from a whole lifestyle that was being lived!

Connections to family, school, work, and new friends all have to be formed again. All of that has to be kept in balance with the things being done to maintain mental health or sobriety—support groups, twelve-step meetings, therapy appointments. Many kids are still involved in the court system, which also takes a lot of time; they're doing community service and attending court dates and probation meetings.

Balance and structure go together. In order to maintain balance, some kind of organization or structure needs to be in place. Many of these kids have never kept a planner or calendar. Part of the support they need is help learning how to get and stay organized. Having structure and keeping balance helps maintain recovery. Sometimes, the opposite is true. Some kids are so obsessive and/or compulsive that learning balance has more to do with letting go. That kind of letting go goes back to learning to think differently.

Relapse

Relapse is when the troubled adolescent slips, falls backward, and feels the need to put the mask back on. Although I hate to admit it, that is likely to happen. There are so many triggers out there that are trying to hook a recovering person and bring her back to her old ways that they are hard to avoid. Learning what those triggers are and how to avoid them is the key to staying in recovery. Support groups, twelve-step meetings, or a good recovery therapist can be very helpful with this.

The risk in a relapse is that she may never come back out from behind the mask again. Not coming out can be caused by shame, fear, and a lot of other things.

"Fuck. Here I am again. I hate it and yet
I love it. How can I go back to everyone

and tell them what I've done? Who are my true friends? They are going to hate me, but my friends will accept me. But do I accept me? Maybe I should just give up. Maybe I should die, but maybe I should live. Fucking confused again."

Honestly, relapse can be a good thing. That quote doesn't make it sound like it, but after the troubled adolescent experiences what life is like when she can really feel again and experience life, it's pretty hard to go back to the fakeness and numbness of wearing that mask. Relapsing proves that life without the mask is so much better than life with it.

No one should give up on the person who relapses! She will have to accept the consequences of what she did, but she should not have to accept the loss of love and support. It may feel like starting over, but she has already learned so much. It has not been forgotten. She can build back up a positive life after a relapse happens much faster because she already learned so much the first time around. A recovering person should never give up! Someone supporting a person in recovery must also never give up.

Sometimes that means doing tough things. I know parents who have had to kick their child out of the house. When such a thing is done with love and an honest explanation, it is a step along the path of recovery. Recovery, in the end, is the choice of the recovering person. Support is necessary, but it has to be accepted for it to be of any value.

The recovering person should just never give up. The life he has during, and after, recovery is so much better than the life behind that mask.

Afterword

Well, today is January 14, 2011 and I have finished my final draft for submission to the publisher. At the start, I said, "It's my hope to pass that knowledge on to you. Whether you are the adolescent yourself or a parent or a friend who just wants to understand better, it is my hope that *Behind the Mask* helps you understand and learn more about helping kids let go of the mask and become the people they were born to be. I hope these quotes and my narrations about those quotes will help you understand more about:

- the despair that lies behind the mask;
- the emotions and behavior that fuel that despair;
- the relationship of the mask to addictions;
- how love and trust leads to hope and recovery; and
- how someone can be the person who makes that recovery possible.

Understanding is only the beginning, so I also hope to help people learn how to deal with these kids and their masks in more helpful and productive ways."

You'll be the judge who decides if I fulfilled my goal. It's not my words that are important. It is your perception of those words that actually matters. I hope it was worth your time and money. Thank you for reading. I would love to hear your response. You can find me on my website at adolescenttherapistmi.com, or email me at dennisrozema@gmail.com

There is one last letter I would like you to read. It was given to me near the person's high school graduation and is very important to me. I hope that sharing this final part explains one last time why it is important to listen to and understand the person living behind the mask.

I have had so many great relationships with so many clients and students. Most of them move on and live out their lives. I know I have been one piece in a puzzle that has helped them see the whole. For me, that is why we are all here: to help each other find the way. Even if we can be just one piece in the puzzle of others' lives, we make a difference.

With some clients and students, however, I know I had more impact. I was a major piece, without which the whole would never have been seen. I have found that those relationships become a piece of my life as well. In the introduction, I talked about learning a lot from those I have worked with. It is because I listened and learned from them as much, if not more, than they listened and learned from me. Each of them has become a piece of me. It is what they have taught me that has allowed me to write this book.

This letter explains better than I can why we need to let go of our masks or help others let go of theirs. As of today, this young lady, who is now in her thirties, is living on her own, sober, and just got married—things that, at one point in her life, she never thought could happen.

> *"Once upon a time, there was a little girl. She was very unhappy and scared on the inside, so she tried to hide it by appearing angry and mean on the outside, which worked. No one really wanted to be her friend, except for some people who were exactly like her. The little girl had no one to try to help her. Then one day, something really bad happened to the little girl, and she was more scared and unhappy than she'd ever been before, so one of her friends took her to meet a nice man. The nice man felt very sorry for this little girl, because she had more unhappiness and confusion than any one little girl could ever handle. So from that day on, the nice man tried to help the little girl. He would listen to her any time she wanted to talk; he never turned her away.*

As time went on, the little girl made a lot of mistakes and did some bad things, but the nice man never gave up on her nor stopped trying to help her. He was the only one who didn't lose his faith in her. And with the nice man's help, the little girl started realizing some important things and making some very important changes, and pretty soon, she wasn't such a little girl anymore.

Then one day, the girl who wasn't quite so little anymore realized that the time had come to say good-bye to the nice man who had helped her for so long. And upon realizing that, she started to think about how many people had come and gone through her life, how many friends she had seen walk out the door, and how she had very few constants. The nice man was one of them. The girl also realized that not many people had confidence in her anymore, she had let them all down, and they had given up on her. The nice man had never given up on her, even during the times when she had given up on herself. She looked at how much she had changed over that time, and she realized that, if it hadn't been for the nice man, she never would have known enough to want to change nor possessed the courage to help her make these changes. And THEN, she realized that if it hadn't been for the changes she had made, she probably would not be here to talk, because she probably would be dead.

And so, upon coming to these realizations, the girl knew that nothing she ever did or said could be enough to thank the nice man for all he had done for her. In fact, she wondered if she could ever even explain to him exactly how much it all meant to her. And so she didn't really try. She knew that nothing she did would ever be enough, and anyway, she was pretty sure that he didn't need to hear her try. She was pretty sure that, since he knew her so well, he also knew how much he meant to her, how grateful she was, and how much she loved him. Because she knew how much he cared about her, and she didn't say that about very many people at all. But the nice man was different. He always had been. And she knew that it didn't matter how long it was until they talked or saw each other again. Because very special friends are like that; they never really leave you, not entirely.

THE END

I honestly do owe you my life, because if it weren't for you, I would not be here to write that today. You forced me to see the things I was determined not to see, and you forced me to see that I needed to change those things in order to be happy. I'm nowhere near perfect, and who I am today is by no means the finished product, but I can say quite confidently that who I am today is a far better and happier person than who I was three years ago or two years ago. A lot of that is because of you. You never told me what to do; you showed me who I could be. You taught me that you should never stop learning and growing, because when you do, you're not really living. Most

importantly, I suppose, you taught me that
it's never too late. And that will stick with
me for the rest of my life.
Because thank you isn't really enough, I
will end this letter with
I love you tons,"

I don't have the words to properly express the gratitude I feel for what this person wrote. I know I'm a pretty emotional person, because it still brings tears to my eyes.

No matter who is reading this book, I hope this proves that anyone can make a difference.

Anyone can make a difference to that person behind the mask, even if it is you living there behind the mask. I urge people to reach out, to care, to listen, to understand. And I ask them to challenge and confront. People need to set examples with their own willingness to trust and share. The troubled adolescent can come from behind the mask, and someone can help bring her out from behind her mask.

People put that mask there because they needed it at a time when they were not able to face the real world. This is now, not then. The world can be what they want it to be here and now, in the present, today. Today, that mask hurts more than it helps.

They should bring their love out from behind the mask and then bring their devotion, their passion, and their tenderness. They should trust again. They should let the mask go. They shouldn't be ashamed if they can't seem to do it on their own. They should ask for help. If it doesn't work, they should ask for help again. They should keep asking until they find what they need. It's out there. They will never find it if they don't look. Don't stop looking!

With knowledge comes understanding
With understanding comes truth
With truth comes love and forgiveness
With love and forgiveness
There is a light that erases the mask

Discussion Guide
For
Behind The Mask

The following pages include Items for Discussion and a page of space to be used for a couple of purposes.

- First – Use the space for keeping notes to yourself about your own particular situation and how you want to make changes in your own life, or help someone else make changes in theirs.
- Second – Questions can be used as a discussion guide for book clubs or other types of groups. I encourage readers to get together and openly discuss "Behind The Mask" and how it can be used to help each other deal with the issues brought up in the book.

Items for Discussion:

1. What do you believe about the concept that all people wear masks? Give an example in your own life when you have worn a mask. Whether you share it or not, this is a good place to start being honest with yourself. What do you keep hidden from others?

2. What is the difference in the masks that most people wear and the masks being talked about in the book?

3.   Use a quote in the book, or a situation from your own life to talk about how masks both help and hurt situations in which we find ourselves.

4. Using what you have learned from the book, and possibly from your own experiences, describe depression and how it develops.

5. What does hurt and pain from the past have to do with how depression develops? Again, this is an opportunity for you to honestly look at yourself or someone you may be concerned about.

6.	The book talks about fear and how it may develop in the past but still influences people in their present lives. Discuss what you have learned about this and what your beliefs are about how this happens.

7.   The chapter on alcohol and drug use has a sub-title that states, "It feels right for a while but it only makes everything worse." Use examples from the book or your own life to support or reject that statement.

8.   What does the book imply about the difficulty in choosing life or choosing death with a depressed person? What are your beliefs about how difficult that may be?

9. Using examples from quotes in the book or from situations in your own life discuss the relationship between the issue of loss of love and the issue of trust.

10. Using information in the chapter on Awareness – Learning to think a new way, discuss the importance of learning to think differently, how easy or hard you believe that is to do, and then give examples from either the book or your own life that support your beliefs.

11. Using examples from the book or from your own life discuss the steps you believe it takes to recover from the type of issues brought up in the book or from the issues you have faced in your life.

12. The sub-title for the chapter on Recovery is "It's a New Beginning, Not the End. What does the book tell you that supports that? Do you agree or disagree? How has this been true in your life?